Dear Parent:

Buckle up! You are about to join your child on a very exciting journey. The destination? Independent reading!

Road to Reading will help you and your child get there. The program offers books at five levels, or Miles, that accompany children from their first attempts at reading to successfully reading on their own. Each Mile is paved with engaging stories and delightful artwork.

Getting Started
For children who know the alphabet and are eager to begin reading
• easy words • fun rhythms • big type • picture clues

Reading With Help
For children who recognize some words and sound out others with help
• short sentences • pattern stories • simple plotlines

Reading On Your Own
For children who are ready to read easy stories by themselves
• longer sentences • more complex plotlines • easy dialogue

First Chapter Books
For children who want to take the plunge into chapter books
• bite-size chapters • short paragraphs • full-color art

Chapter Books
For children who are comfortable reading independently
• longer chapters • occasional black-and-white illustrations

There's no need to hurry through the Miles. Road to Reading is designed without age or grade levels. Children can progress at their own speed, developing confidence and pride in their reading ability no matter what their age or grade.

So sit back and enjoy t!

D1365434

To Samosaurus, Cassieraptor,
and Lukieopteryx
S.A.

To Max and Gray Kitty,
my great pets
N.E.

Library of Congress Cataloging-in-Publication Data
Albee, Sarah.
My new pet is the greatest / by Sarah Albee ; illustrated by Nate Evans.
p. cm. — (Road to reading. Mile 2)
Summary: When Sam brings home a baby dinosaur, his new pet's size
and boisterous antics create unusual problems for the family.
ISBN 0-307-26208-1 (pbk.)
[1. Dinosaurs—Fiction. 2. Pets—Fiction.] I. Evans, Nate, ill.
II. Title. III. Series.
PZ7.A3174Myn   1999
[E]—dc21   98-8772
                                                    CIP
                                                    AC

A GOLDEN BOOK • **New York**
Golden Books Publishing Company, Inc. New York, New York 10106

ISBN: 0-307-26208-1   R MMI

My New Pet is the GREATEST

by Sarah Albee
illustrated by Nate Evans

Last week
I got a new pet.

"He followed me home,"
I told my parents.
"Can I keep him?"

I named him Al.

Al is so smart.

He can play catch.

8

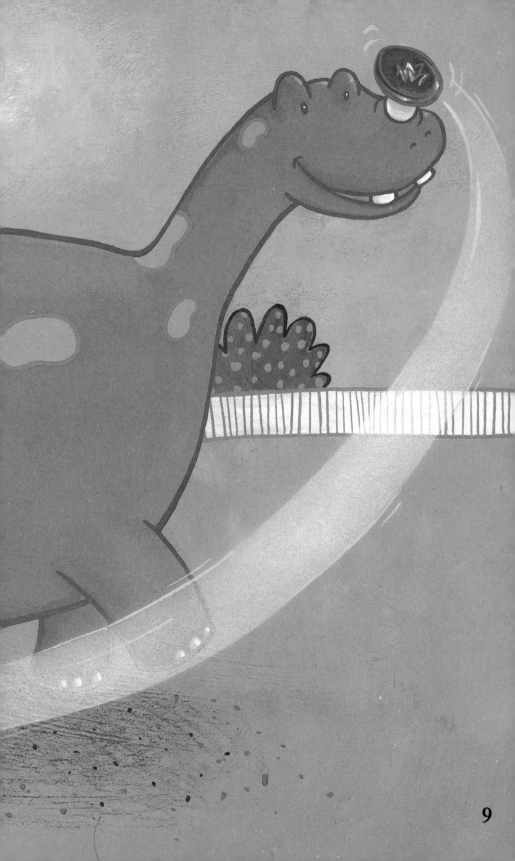

He can roll over.

He can even fetch
Dad's slippers.

12

Al tries hard to be good.
But yesterday
he chased the neighbor's cat.

And then
he buried his bones
in Mom's flower garden.

And then
he scared the mailman.

But that wasn't Al's fault.
Al was just trying
to be friendly.

19

It isn't always easy
taking care of Al.

I have to feed him every day.

I have to give him baths.

I have to take him
for walks.

24

And, of course,
I have to clean up
after him.

But it's worth it.
Al is a great pet.

Mom and Dad think so, too.
There's no doubt about it—
Al is part
of the family now.